Migrating Animals of the Water

by Susan Labella

Reading consultant:
Susan Nations, M.Ed.
author, literacy coach, and consultant in literacy development

Science and curriculum consultant:
Debra Voege, M.A.
science and math curriculum resource teacher

WEEKLY READER®
PUBLISHING

Please visit our web site at: www.garethstevens.com
For a free color catalog describing our list of high-quality books,
call 1-800-542-2595 (USA) or 1-800-387-3178 (Canada).

Library of Congress Cataloging-in-Publication Data available upon request from publisher.

ISBN-13: 978-0-8368-8419-7 (lib. bdg.)
ISBN-10: 0-8368-8419-1 (lib. bdg.)
ISBN-13: 978-0-8368-8424-1 (softcover)
ISBN-10: 0-8368-8424-8 (softcover)

This edition first published in 2008 by
Weekly Reader® Books
An imprint of Gareth Stevens Publishing
1 Reader's Digest Road
Pleasantville, NY 10570-7000 USA

Photo credits: Cover: © Photodisc/Business & Industry, Vol.1; p.4-21: © Photodisc/Techno Finance; cover: Natalie Fobes/Corbis; p.4-5: Image State/Jupiter Images; p.6: Jeff Rotman/ Getty Images; p.7: David Nunuk/Getty Images; p.8: AFP/Getty Images; p.9 SeaPics; p.11: Digital Vision/Getty Images; p.12: Paul Jenkins/Animals Animals; p.13: Kami Strunsee/ © Weekly Reader Early Learning Library; p.14: Bruce Watkins/Animals Animals; p.15: Frans Lanting/Minden Pictures; p.17: Natalie Fobes/Corbis; p.18: Leigh Haeger for Weekly Reader; p.20: SeaPics; p.21: Leigh Haeger for Weekly Reader

Printed in the United States of America

1 2 3 4 5 6 7 8 9 11 10 09 08 07

Table of Contents

Cover and title page: Salmon swim over long distances to get back to the place where they were hatched.

Why Do Animals Migrate?

Underneath the surface of the world's waters, animals of all sorts—huge to tiny—are on the move. They are taking part in **migrations**.

Migration is a regular journey from one place to another. Most animals migrate to find food, to mate and have young, or to find a better climate.

Some animals migrate very long distances. Some very small animals may migrate only a very short distance. Migrating animals can take months or a lifetime to complete their journeys. Gray whales spend months traveling. Salmon put their whole life into a migration. Some creatures make a round-trip journey once each night.

Sea turtles are long-distance migrators.

Chapter 1

Migration Mysteries

How are some fish and reptiles able to locate a faraway place that will give them the food they need to grow and mature? How do some adult fish find their way hundreds or thousands of miles to the very spot where they hatched? What guides great white sharks to seal breeding grounds to catch **prey**? Why do some ocean mammals follow a pattern of leaving cold waters for warm waters in order to mate and give birth?

Sharks swim many miles to find food.

Those are all mysteries of migration. Scientists are not always sure what signals water animals to migrate or where to go. Experts think temperature, the amount of daylight, or animals' **internal clocks** may let them know when to set out on their journeys. Once these animals set out, experts say wind directions, water currents, and even a sense of smell may guide them along their way.

Salmon returning to their home streams to **spawn**, or lay eggs, can face predators such as eagles, bears, and wildcats.

Recently, millions of giant jellyfish have been migrating to the Sea of Japan. Experts want to know why. Some think the 6-foot (2 meter) wide, 400-pound (181 kilogram) animals have drifted on ocean currents from waters near China. Others think seas heated by global warming have caused the jellyfish to breed more and have increased their numbers near Japan. These giants are causing problems. They get caught in fishing nets, leaving little room for fish that people want to catch.

The giant jellyfish swim by sucking water into their bodies and then squeezing it out in a stream. They also drift on strong ocean currents.

Spiny lobsters live on the ocean floor in shallow waters. They hide in coral reefs during the day and come out at night to feed. In the fall, as temperatures drop, large groups of lobsters migrate to warmer waters. The prickly-looking lobsters follow a leader, walking in **queues**, or straight lines along the bottom of the sea. The antenna of each lobster touches the lobster ahead of it to stay connected to the group.

Lobsters take turns being the leader of the line. It is as if the lobsters know they must share the work.

9

Chapter 2

In Search of Food

Usually great white sharks near California swim along the coast to hunt for seals or sea lions to eat. Recently, scientists who study the 2,500-pound (1,134 kg) sharks learned that these animals travel much farther than anyone had thought. As winter approaches, the sharks migrate out to deep ocean waters and stay there for several months.

While out at sea, great white sharks make many deep dives.

One shark migrated about 2,200 miles (3,500 kilometers) to Hawaii, remaining there all winter and spring! Why do the sharks migrate to deeper waters? Scientists say it could be for mating or for a change in food.

Many great white sharks also live off the coast of South Africa. Scientists tracked one named Nicole that swam a record 12,400 miles (almost 20,000 kilometers) from South Africa to Australia and back!

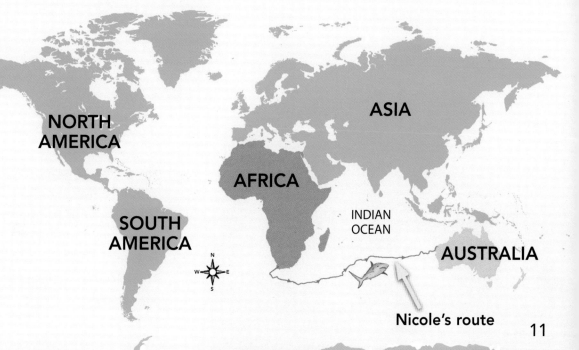

Nicole's route

Chapter 3

A Safe Place for Babies

Many animals migrate to find safe places to bear and raise their young. They may make long journeys and leave places where there is plenty of food to do that. Gray whales spend summers in the cold waters of the Bering Sea, feeding on tiny **krill**, or small shrimp-like animals. The Bering Sea is a great source of food. The whales build up **blubber**, or fat,

Gray whales swim about 3,000 to 4,000 miles (4800 to 6400 kilometers) to reach warm-water lagoons! The long return trip is made by mother *and* baby!

that gives them energy they will need for their migration. In October, groups of gray whales set out. They leave the cold waters and swim south to warm-water **lagoons** in Mexico. The whales swim for two to three months to reach the safe lagoons. There is less food in the lagoons, but the warm water is comfortable for the animals to have their babies. In the spring the whales leave, returning north to their cold-water feeding grounds. They feast there all summer, building up the blubber they need to migrate again in the fall.

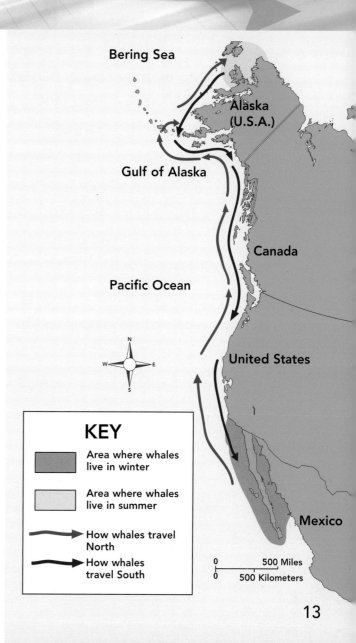

Bering Sea

Alaska (U.S.A.)

Gulf of Alaska

Canada

Pacific Ocean

United States

N
W ● E
S

Mexico

KEY

Area where whales live in winter

Area where whales live in summer

→ How whales travel North

➤ How whales travel South

0   500 Miles
0   500 Kilometers

13

Northern elephant seals migrate twice a year and travel up to 21,000 miles (33,800 kilometers) altogether! In January, females give birth to pups on islands off the coast of California or Mexico. By March, the adult seals leave the young to grow up on their own. The adult seals return to northeast Pacific waters to feed. By the summer, after getting their fill of tasty treats such as squid and shellfish, the seals migrate south to the islands again. This time they **molt**,

Northern elephant seals travel up to 21,000 miles (33,800 km) during their double migrations.

or lose a layer of skin and fur. After molting, the seals swim north again. They feed again, diving deep in the cold waters, until it is time to start their cycle of double migration again.

Elephant seals go ashore to molt. After molting, they gradually grow new layers of skin and fur.

Chapter 4

Lifelong Travelers

Some animals spend their whole lives on a migration. Most fish live either in salt water or fresh water. Salmon spend their lives in both. Young salmon hatch in cold, freshwater streams. They spend several months to a year there eating insects and growing. Then the young fish, called **smolts**, swim to ocean waters. Here, they spend one to five years, feeding and migrating over thousands of saltwater miles. When full grown, they leave the ocean to return to their home streams. The salmon must be able to recognize the smells they learned as smolts, which will guide them to their "home waters." The journey of a salmon to its home waters can be quite a struggle. They have to fight their way upstream in strong currents. They sometimes have to leap out of the water to jump over obstacles. Predators such as bears sit by the streams waiting to snatch up the migrants.

The fish use the last of their energy to **spawn** in their home streams—then they die. In a few months new salmon will hatch to begin the cycle again.

Young salmon are called smolts. They spend several years living in the ocean.

Loggerhead sea turtles hatch from nests on beaches from North Carolina to Florida. The newborns make a dash for the sea. The one to two-inch **hatchlings** swim out as fast as they can. A powerful ocean current passes close to the eastern coast of the United States. This stream of water carries the turtles out to the Sargasso Sea. This "sea" is really a slow-moving area of water with a huge mass of seaweed growing at the center. Warm water and plenty of food make this a perfect place for the hatchlings to grow. Some turtles stay ten years.

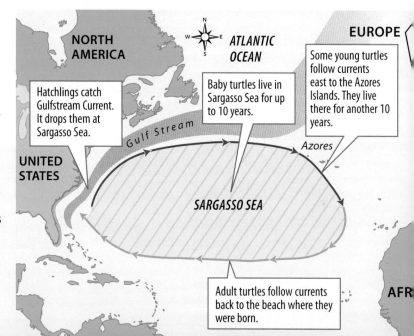

Lifetime Migration of the Loggerhead Turtles

NORTH AMERICA

ATLANTIC OCEAN

EUROPE

Some young turtles follow currents east to the Azores Islands. They live there for another 10 years.

Hatchlings catch Gulfstream Current. It drops them at Sargasso Sea.

Baby turtles live in Sargasso Sea for up to 10 years.

Gulf Stream

Azores

UNITED STATES

SARGASSO SEA

Adult turtles follow currents back to the beach where they were born.

AFR

KEY

Nesting grounds of loggerhead turtles

Many sea turtles then continue east on the current, gathering near the Azores islands off Portugal. Later, they will pick up another current and travel west across the Atlantic. They will return to home waters to feed and become adults. When the females are 20- to 30-years old, they will mate and lay their eggs—on the same beach where they themselves once hatched.

A new batch of hatchlings will now rush to sea.

The Sargasso Sea is a stopping place for other migrating animals, too. Some eels begin life here as **larvae**. The larvae drift with the current for about three years. As they go, they change into tiny see-through eels, called glass eels.

Reaching Europe, many of the eels swim miles up freshwater rivers to feed and grow. During the next ten to fourteen years, the eels become full size.

Then they begin a migration back to the Sargasso Sea. The determined eels will travel for hours over land if it blocks their way to the ocean. Groups of eels, now a silver color, reach the Sargasso to mate. After mating and laying eggs, the grown eels die. New larvae hatch and begin another long journey.

Spotlight: The Sargasso Sea

The salty Sargasso Sea in the middle of the North Atlantic Ocean has fast-moving water currents surrounding it. The sea's warm water makes a good home for some animals.

Scientists say a daily migration takes place in the Sargasso Sea. Each night, a swarm of millions of tiny animals migrates at one time. The swarm is made up of tiny shrimp-like krill, baby crabs, and baby eels. It is also made up of some creatures that can only be seen with a microscope.

Krill is a shrimp-like animal that some whales and other ocean creatures eat.

These animals form a thick, carpet-like layer under the sea. At night, the layer rises to the surface so the animals can feed on small plants at the water's surface. By morning, the layer migrates back to the deep. Scientists think this **vertical migration** occurs at night so the animals can avoid predators.

Animals such as krill, crab larvae, and snails without shells migrate up and down in the Sargasso Sea.

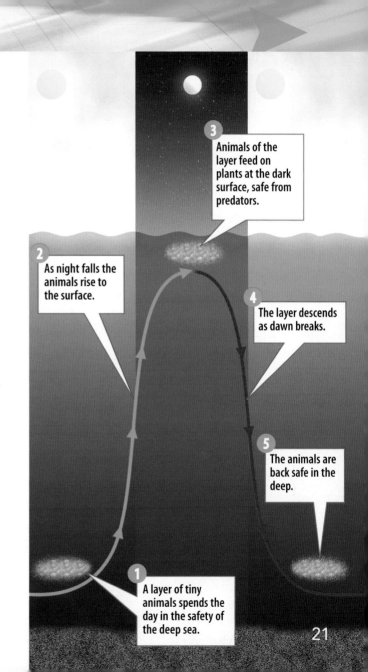

3 Animals of the layer feed on plants at the dark surface, safe from predators.

2 As night falls the animals rise to the surface.

4 The layer descends as dawn breaks.

5 The animals are back safe in the deep.

1 A layer of tiny animals spends the day in the safety of the deep sea.

21

Glossary

blubber—fat that is found between the skin and muscle of marine mammals

hatchling—a newly hatched bird, amphibian, fish or reptile

internal clock—internal signals that tell an animal's brain when to eat, sleep, migrate and so on

lagoon—a shallow body of water separated from the sea

molt—to shed an outer covering and have it replaced by a new growth

prey—an animal caught for food

queue—a long line

smolt—young salmon when it is covered with silvery scales and first migrates to the sea

spawn—to deposit eggs

vertical migration—migration that follows an up and down path

For More Information

Books

Animals That Migrate. Animals (series).
   Carmen Bredeson (Franklin Watts)

Animals Migrating: How, When, Where, and Why Animals Migrate.
   Animal Behavior. Etta Kaner (Kids Can Press Ltd.)

Think of an Eel. Karen Walker (Read and Wonder)

Web Sites

**Journey North: A Global Study
of Wildlife Migration and Seasonal Change**

http://www.learner.org/jnorth/

Find out how changes in the seasons affect animals.
Track migration routes, see maps, and lots more!

BrainPOP Jr. Migration

http://www.brainpopjr.com/science/animals/migration/

Try a few of these migration activities at home with your family.

Index

About the Author

Susan Labella has been a teacher and an editor of children's publications. She remembers watching wild geese fly south for the winter and wondering how they knew where to go! Today Susan enjoys writing books for children.